THE GREAT™
AMERICAN
HISTORY
QUIZ

The Presidents

THE GREAT™
AMERICAN
HISTORY
QUIZ

The Presidents

Series Created by
Abbe Raven and Dana Calderwood

Written by
**Charles Nordlander, Howard Blumenthal, Dana Calderwood and
Robert Sharenow, with additional questions by John Aherne**

WARNER BOOKS

A Time Warner Company

Copyright ©2001 by A&E Television.
The History Channel, the "H" logo, and the Great American History Quiz are trademarks of A&E Television and are registered in the United States and other countries. All rights reserved.

Warner Books, Inc., 1271 Avenue of the Americas,
New York, NY 10020

Visit our Web site at www.twbookmark.com

For information on Time Warner Trade Publishing's
online publishing program, visit www.ipublish.com

 A Time Warner Company

Printed in the United States of America

First Printing: June 2001
10 9 8 7 6 5 4 3 2 1

Library of Congress Cataloging-in-Publication Data

    The great American history quiz III : the presidents.
      p. cm.
    ISBN 0-446-67686-1
    1. Presidents—United States—History—Examinations, questions,
etc. 2. Presidents—United States—History—Miscellanea. I. Title:
Great American history quiz 3. II. History Channel (Television
network).

    E176.1.G817   2001
    973—dc21   2001017927

Cover design by Carolyn Lechter
Cover photographs by Corbis/Time Pix
Book design and text composition by Ralph Fowler

This edition of **The Great American History Quiz** will test your knowledge of American presidents. **Not** only do the presidents of this great nation make good leaders, but they also make for some good trivia. Case in point: James Madison was only five feet, six inches tall. Imagine him and Lincoln back to back! William Harrison was president for only one month; after that . . . he was mostly dead. Harding: first inauguration on radio. While we're on the subject, here are a few other presidential firsts . . .

Let's start off with an easy one: Who was the first president of the United States?

(a) George Washington

(b) John Adams

(c) George Bush

(d) John Hanson

A N S W E R

Although conventional wisdom has it that George Washington was the first president of the United States, a case could be made for that honor going to choice **(d)** John Hanson. When the Articles of Confederation were adopted on March 1, 1781, John Hanson was unanimously elected by Congress to run the young country.

2 Who was the first president to be defeated for re-election?

(a) George Washington

(b) John Quincy Adams

(c) John Adams

(d) George Bush

ANSWER

The answer is **(c)** John Adams—our nation's second president. He was defeated by Thomas Jefferson in 1800. But it didn't take long for the Adams family to make it back to the presidency: Twenty-four years later, John Quincy Adams became the first son of a president to follow in his father's footsteps.

3 While we're on the subject of firsts, here's a question about first names: There has been only one president named Ulysses, just one named Zachary, and only one named Abraham. But what is the most common first name among our presidents?

(a) William

(b) John

(c) James

(d) Thomas

3

A N S W E R

The answer is **(c)**: There have been six presidents named James—Madison, Monroe, Polk, Buchanan, Garfield, and Carter. The names John and William are tied for second place, with four presidents each. The most recent William, of course, is William Jefferson Clinton.

4 In order to become president of the United States, you must be born on native soil. However, although all of our early presidents were born in America, they weren't all born U.S. citizens. The question is, who was the first president to be born a U.S. citizen?

(a) Andrew Jackson

(b) Martin Van Buren

(c) Franklin Pierce

(d) John Adams

A N S W E R

The answer is **(b)** Martin Van Buren, our eighth president. His seven predecessors—including Washington, Adams, Jefferson—were all born before the United States existed, so they were born British subjects. Now, isn't that interesting?

5 Van Buren is also famous for another first. What is it?

(a) The first (and only) president who was formerly Speaker of the House

(b) The first to keep all of his campaign promises

(c) The first president to employ the now standard "Hail to the Chief" song at his inauguration

(d) The first to host the now annual Thanksgiving dinner at the White House

(c). The first time "Hail to the Chief" was played to announce the arrival of a president was at Martin Van Buren's inauguration in 1837. All of the other answers, incidentally, were things that James K. Polk did first. Most notably he kept all of his campaign promises: He gained control of the entire Oregon Territory, he fought to make Texas a part of the United States, and he did not seek a second term.

6 Who was the first president to ask Congress for a declaration of war?

(a) James Madison

(b) James Polk

(c) Abraham Lincoln

(d) John Adams

6

ANSWER

(a). James Madison was the first president to ask Congress for a declaration of war. His request was granted, and so America entered into the War of 1812 against England.

7 Who was the first vice president to take the presidential office due to the death of the president?

(a) John Tyler

(b) John Quincy Adams

(c) Chester A. Arthur

(d) Franklin Pierce

A N S W E R

(a). John Tyler succeeded William Henry Harrison in 1841, after Harrison had died of pneumonia one month after being inaugurated.

8 Who was the first president to set up a Christmas tree in the White House?

(a) George Washington

(b) Franklin Pierce

(c) Grover Cleveland

(d) James Buchanan

8

ANSWER

(b). Franklin Pierce was the first president to introduce the Christmas tree to the White House: He did it in 1856 for a group of Washington Sunday school children. The first national Christmas tree, however, was lit in the year 1923 on the White House lawn by President Calvin Coolidge.

9 The presidential election of 1912 was the first in which:

(a) The winner lost the majority of the popular votes

(b) The winner lost the majority of electoral votes

(c) Women could vote

(d) A former president ran against an incumbent—and both lost to a third candidate

ANSWER

Talk about too many cooks! The answer is **(d)**: In the 1912 election Theodore Roosevelt, William Howard Taft, the incumbent, and Woodrow Wilson were all vying for the title commander in chief. Although Wilson won only 42 percent of the popular vote, he won 435 electoral votes. To this day, many people resent Roosevelt for splitting the Republican vote when he entered the race as a Progressive party candidate.

10 Who was the first president whose inauguration was broadcast on national television?

(a) Harry Truman

(b) Dwight D. Eisenhower

(c) Franklin Roosevelt

(d) John F. Kennedy

ANSWER

(a). The 1949 inauguration of President Harry Truman was the first to be televised on national TV.

11 Theodore Roosevelt was a man of many firsts. He was the first president to be a Scout master, the first president to have a stuffed animal named after him, and the first to announce his candidacy for president in Las Vegas. But there's more! Which of the following is *not* one of Roosevelt's firsts?

(a) The first president to win the Nobel prize

(b) The first president to ride in an airplane

(c) The first Phi Beta Kappa to be named president

(d) The first to publish a book while in office

ANSWER

All of the above can be said of Roosevelt except for **(c)**. John Quincy Adams was actually the first Phi Beta Kappa to be elected president.

Remember when John F. Kennedy was president, and some misguided fools proclaimed him the youngest president ever? We know, as do most of you, that Theodore Roosevelt was the youngest ever American president. JFK was, however, the youngest man to be elected president, as Teddy Roosevelt was sworn in as president after the death of President McKinley. And Kennedy was definitely the first president whose movie-star looks helped make him a favorite with female voters. That's why we affectionately call this category Ich Bin ein Babe Magnet.

12 During the televised debates between JFK and Richard Nixon, Kennedy promised a New Frontier. Later, he delivered on that promise with programs like the Peace Corps. Some say that Kennedy won the presidency because he looked and sounded great on television—while the opposite was true for Nixon. The question is, how many times did these candidates debate?

(a) 1   (c) 4

(b) 2   (d) 6

A N S W E R

The answer is **(c)**: They debated four times. But Kennedy's terrific performance didn't translate into a landslide victory. He won by fewer than 120,000 votes, a razor-thin margin of less than two-tenths of one percent of the total popular vote.

13 Prior to his presidency, Kennedy's personal accomplishments included a best-selling analysis of England prior to World War II and a Pulitzer prize-winning book about U.S. senators. Name his 1957 Pulitzer prize-winning best-seller.

(a) *Why England Slept*

(b) *PT 109*

(c) *Profiles in Courage*

(d) *Moby Dick*

ANSWER

The answer is **(c)** *Profiles in Courage.* It's about courageous acts by U.S. senators, and it was written by Kennedy while he recuperated from a back injury. That injury was related to Kennedy's heroic rescue of ten crewmen under his command aboard the torpedo boat PT 109.

14 Freedom was an important theme of Kennedy's administration: freedom for Black Americans in their struggle for civil rights and freedom from Communism abroad. While visiting the Berlin Wall in 1963, JFK delivered a speech about freedom and spoke these famous words: "All free men, wherever they may live, are citizens of Berlin. And therefore, as a free man, I take pride in the words '*Ich bin ein Berliner.*'" Kennedy, of course, thought he was saying "I am a Berliner." But what was the actual translation of his words?

(a) "I am an airliner"

(b) "It smells in Berlin"

(c) "I am a jelly doughnut"

(d) "I was a Berliner"

14

ANSWER

(c). Yes, JFK really said "I am a jelly dough-nut." Here's what happened: *"Ich bin Berliner"* means "I'm a Berliner." But Kennedy said *"Ich bin EIN Berliner,"* which changed the meaning considerably. We'd like to think he laughed at his mistake.

Some presidents are better known by their nick-names than by their actual names. So for the next few questions, we'll give you a nickname, and you decide whether that nickname pertains to a U.S. president . . . or a rap star.

The first name is "Great Hammerer" —is that a presidential nickname or a rap star?

(a) U.S. president

(b) Rap star

ANSWER

"Great Hammerer" was the presidential nickname of Ulysses S. Grant.

16 Next, what about "Big Willie": Is he a U.S. president or a rap star?

(a) U.S. president

(b) Rap star

16

"Big Willie" is rap and movie star Will Smith. You might remember him as the Fresh Prince of Bel-Air.

17 Now check out this name: "Handsome Frank." Does that sound like a presidential nickname or a rap star?

(a) U.S. president

(b) Rap star

ANSWER

Harry Truman called him "the best-looking president the White House ever had." He was talking about Franklin Pierce, whose nickname was "Handsome Frank."

18 "Sharp Knife"?

(a) U.S. president

(b) Rap star

18

ANSWER

"Sharp Knife" was the name given to Andrew Jackson by the Indians he subdued during the 1817 Seminole War.

19 Here's one more name: "Ol' Dirty Bastard." Does it refer to a president or a rap star?

(a) U.S. president

(b) Rap star

ANSWER

Rap star "Ol' Dirty Bastard" was a member of the Wu-Tang Clan. But give yourself credit if you said president. At least one president must have been called this, though never out loud.

Presidents will say anything to get elected. To be president, you have to be willing to tell different versions of the truth to different groups of voters. (We'd call them lies if they didn't come out of the mouths of politicians.) So let's look back at some famous—and infamous—presidential campaign slogans to see whether the men we elected made good on their promises.

20 In 1928 Republicans helped Herbert Hoover win the election with that famous promise of "a chicken in every pot." But a few years later, most Americans were thinking "Hey Herb, how about if we stuff you in a pot?" What was the second half of that famous Republican campaign slogan?

(a) "a stove to cook it on"

(b) "a car in every backyard"

(c) "and wine in every glass"

(d) "a job for every man"

20

ANSWER

(b). The Republicans promised "a chicken in every pot, a car in every backyard." They didn't count on the Great Depression, which delivered widespread poverty instead.

21 One of the most memorable campaign slogans was "Tippecanoe and Tyler too!" William Henry Harrison used it to defeat which Democrat in the 1840 election?

(a) Andrew Jackson

(b) James K. Polk

(c) John Quincy Adams

(d) Martin Van Buren

A N S W E R

(d). William Harrison beat incumbent president Martin Van Buren in the 1840 election. Incidentally, "Tippecanoe" does not refer to boat-tipping. Rather, it was the site of General Harrison's victory against the legendary Shawnee Indian chief Tecumsech in 1811. And "Tyler," by the way, was Harrison's running mate, John Tyler.

22 When Democrat Woodrow Wilson ran for his second term as president, he campaigned on the slogan "He kept us out of war." Well, that may have been true for his first term, but before he left the presidency, America had entered World War I. Roughly how long after his election did Wilson break his promise?

(a) Five months

(b) Fourteen months

(c) Two years

(d) Three years

ANSWER

(a). Wilson was re-elected on November 7, 1916. Five months later, on April 6, the United States declared war against Germany.

23 "Read my lips: No new taxes." We all remember George Bush's famous pledge. But give him credit—he did better than Wilson and his war. George may have raised taxes, but at least we weren't getting shot at! After winning the election, how long did it take Bush to break his campaign promise?

(a) One year

(b) Two years

(c) Three years

(d) Two months

A N S W E R

The answer is **(b)** two years. Bush won the November 1988 election. And the voters lost when he signed a bill raising taxes in November of 1990. Michael Dukakis, the Democratic candidate who lost the election to Bush, said, "I told the truth and I paid the price."

24 Whose presidential campaign slogan was "Ma, Ma, where's my Pa? Gone to the White House, ha, ha, ha"?

(a) Abraham Lincoln

(b) James Blaine

(c) Henry Clay

(d) Warren G. Harding

24

(b). Smear campaigns are not a twentieth-century invention. "Ma, Ma, where's my Pa? Gone to the White House, ha, ha, ha" was used by supporters of James Blaine in the 1884 election. The slogan was a reference to Grover Cleveland's illegitimate son. But Cleveland didn't take this jab lying down. One of his campaign slogans for that election: "Blaine, Blaine, James G. Blaine, the continental liar from the state of Maine."

25 Finish this more positive and upbeat Democratic campaign slogan: "We Polked you in 1844; we shall _____ in 1852."

(a) Ruin your Whigs

(b) Pierce

(c) Make it Taylor made

(d) Overcome

25

(b). Pierce. Democrat James Polk won the presidency in 1844, and when he decided not to run for re-election in '48 due to poor health, Whig party candidate Zachary Taylor won a close race. The Democrats came up with this zippy slogan for their man Franklin Pierce in 1852.

If you've picked up this book, chances are that you really know your history. But you probably frequently confuse our nation's vice presidents with the roster of the 1962 New York Mets—modern baseball's losingest team. In our next category, we'll name two men—one a U.S. vice president, the other a player on the '62 Mets. You have to identify which one was a VP.

26 Now coming to bat: One man served as vice president during William McKinley's first term; the other was a just-plain-awful catcher for the Mets. Can you name the VP?

(a) Garret Hobart

(b) Hobert Landrith

26

The answer is **(a)**. Garret A. Hobart was McKinley's vice president. Hobie Landrith suffered the indignity of being the first player traded away from the '62 Mets.

27 Next in the lineup: vice president number 31, and Hoover's second in command. The other guy was a Met player with a colorful nickname. So, who was the VP?

(a) Clarence Coleman

(b) Charles Curtis

ANSWER

(b). Charles Curtis watched Herbert Hoover lead the country into the Great Depression. "Depression" also describes how Mets fans felt about Clarence "Choo Choo" Coleman's batting average: One season he hit .178. Now that's depressing.

28 Now at the plate: One man won the Nobel Peace prize and was vice president under Coolidge. The other guy once got called out on a triple when he forgot to touch first base. Tell me who was the VP.

(a) Charles G. Dawes

(b) Marvin E. Throneberry

A N S W E R

The answer is **(a)**. The distinguished
Charles Dawes was our nation's thirtieth
vice president. "Marvelous" Marvin Throneberry was the Met who missed first base.
When Met manager Casey Stengel argued
the call, the ump told him that Marv had
missed second base too. To quote Casey
Stengel: "Can't anybody here play this game?"

Robert Lincoln, Abe's son, was present at three presidential assassinations. Now, four U.S. presidents have been assassinated. At least six more escaped assassins. That's ten attempts on forty-some-odd presidents. So if you're thinking about becoming the big cheese, your odds of getting shot at are about one in four. The odds are even greater if you find Robert Lincoln standing next to you. Here are a few questions about presidential assassinations.

29 Dateline: September 6, 1901. A drifter named Leon Czolgosz grips a loaded gun beneath a handkerchief. With cold-blooded calculation, he approaches President William McKinley on a receiving line in Buffalo, New York. As McKinley moves to shake his hand, Czolgosz fires twice at point-blank range. The president, mortally wounded, shouts unlikely words after he's hit. What were they?

(a) "Somebody get Ida's hat"

(b) "I'm not hit"

(c) "Don't let them hurt him"

(d) "What time is it? What time is it?"

29

The answer is **(c)**. In a startling moment of humanity, McKinley shouted, "Don't let them hurt him" as Czolgosz was viciously beaten after the shooting. Eight days later McKinley was dead. And Czolgosz showed no remorse. After his execution, his corpse was doused in sulfuric acid to speed up decomposition.

30 Dateline: November 1, 1950. The afternoon calm is shattered by the sounds of gunfire, as Oscar Collazo and Griselio Torresola brazenly storm President Truman's temporary residence at Blair House. A bloody gun battle rages, leaving Torresola and a security guard dead. Two other guards are wounded and Collazo takes a bullet in the chest. Thankfully, President Truman isn't hurt, but one question remains unanswered: What provoked this brutal attack?

(a) U.S. immigration policy

(b) Puerto Rican nationalism

(c) U.S. involvement in Southeast Asia

(d) Nuclear testing at Alamogordo, New Mexico

30

The answer is **(b)**. Collazo and Torresola were committed Puerto Rican nationalists who wanted to end U.S. rule of their homeland.

31 Dateline: September 5, 1975. Gerald Ford waves pleasantly to a crowd in Sacramento, unaware that his life is in danger. A petite woman with murder on her mind approaches the president, unnoticed. Then, without warning, Lynette "Squeaky" Fromme pulls out a deadly .45 caliber automatic. Instantly, a bodyguard grabs the arm of the would-be assassin, and the gun drops from her hand. No shots are fired, but the mystery remains: Why did Squeaky Fromme want to kill Gerald Ford?

(a) To draw attention to Charles Manson

(b) To protest the pardon of Richard Nixon

(c) To promote the Symbionese Liberation Army

(d) To protest President Ford's endorsement of the Helsinki Accord

31

A N S W E R

The answer is **(a)**. Squeaky Fromme was a devoted follower of Charles Manson. She hoped that during her trial, Manson would be called as a witness, enabling him to spread his message to the world.

32 But Squeaky Fromme wasn't the only one with an ax to grind with President Ford. On a subsequent trip to California, another attempt was made on his life. What was the name of this second would-be assassin?

(a) Rebecca Oliver

(b) Donald DeFreeze

(c) Sara Jane Moore

(d) Elaine Noble

32

(c). Sara Jane Moore. Though she fired a .38 caliber revolver at Ford, a nearby bystander slapped Mrs. Moore's arm before the gun went off, causing the bullet to go astray.

33 An attempt was made on President Ronald Reagan's life on March 30, 1981. His assailant was John W. Hinkley Jr., a twenty-five-year-old resident of Colorado. During his trial, it emerged that one of Hinkley's motives for shooting the president was to grab the attention of what female celebrity?

(a) Jodie Foster

(b) Cybill Shepherd

(c) Sissy Spacek

(d) Yoko Ono

33

A N S W E R

(a). Inspired by the 1976 movie *Taxi Driver*, in which Robert De Niro plays a character who tries to grab Cybill Shepherd's attention by attempting to assassinate a presidential candidate, John Hinkley Jr. tried to pique the interest of Jodie Foster—who also starred in the movie—by shooting Ronald Reagan.

34 Which of the following presidents was not the victim of an assassination attempt?

(a) Andrew Jackson

(b) Franklin Roosevelt

(c) Ulysses S. Grant

(d) James A. Garfield

ANSWER

(c). No one tried to take the life of Ulysses S. Grant while he was in office. Ironically, he was invited to attend Ford's Theatre with President and Mrs. Lincoln the night Lincoln was shot, but he had declined the invitation.

Presidents have been married to more E-women than any other letter. We've had three first ladies named Elizabeth, two Ediths, two Ellens, one Eleanor, and an Eliza. So here are a few questions about our favorite First Ladies.

35 Mary Todd Lincoln's White House years were filled with incredible tragedy. One son died and another became critically ill. She was accused of being a Confederate traitor, and her husband, of course, was assassinated. But that's not all: Mary's misfortunes continued in later years. Which of the following happened after she had left the White House?

(a) She sold clothing and jewelry to raise cash

(b) Her son had her declared legally insane

(c) Frederick Douglass was asked to give benefit lectures on her behalf

(d) All of the above

35

The answer is **(d)**. Mrs. Lincoln had spent herself into a mountain of debt. Her sale of clothes and jewelry raised little cash, while benefit lectures by Frederick Douglass never went forward. And though her son had her declared insane, a judge overturned the ruling—but not before Mary Lincoln had spent four months in a mental institution.

36 While it is necessary for a president to be born on American soil, there is no such provision for the First Lady. Which was good news for this nineteenth-century president, whose wife is the only First Lady not to be born in America. Which president married a foreign-born woman?

(a) John Quincy Adams

(b) Andrew Jackson

(c) John Tyler

(d) James Buchanan

36

ANSWER

(a). In 1797 John Quincy Adams married Louisa Catherine Johnson, who was born and raised in London.

37 Who is the only president ever to have been divorced?

(a) Ronald Reagan

(b) Richard Nixon

(c) James A. Garfield

(d) William McKinley

A N S W E R

(a). Although several presidents were widowers, Ronald Reagan is the only president to ever have been divorced. He divorced his first wife, Jane Wyman, in 1948, after eight years of marriage.

38 President Reagan may be the only president to have been divorced, but this president's marriage to a divorcée caused a major scandal and accusations of bigamy. Who was it?

(a) Jimmy Carter

(b) John Tyler

(c) Andrew Jackson

(d) Thomas Jefferson

38

ANSWER

(c). When Andrew Jackson married Rachel Donelson Robards in 1791, neither of them were aware that her divorce from her first husband, Lewis Robards, was not yet finalized. Jackson and his wife remarried in 1794, after the divorce was made final. Sadly, Mrs. Jackson never saw her husband enter the White House. She died after he was elected but before his inauguration.

39

Who was the third (and last) First Lady to die during her husband's administration?

(a) Margaret Smith Taylor

(b) Caroline Scott Harrison

(c) Anna Symmes Harrison

(d) Ellen Axson Wilson

39

ANSWER

(d). Ellen Axson Wilson was the third and most recent First Lady to die during her husband's administration.

40 John Philip Sousa himself conducted "The Wedding March" for the only president ever married at the White House. He was twenty-seven years older—and at least a hundred pounds heavier—than his new bride. When asked why he had waited so long to marry, he answered, "I was waiting for my wife to grow up!" At twenty-one years old, she became our nation's youngest First Lady. Grateful women across the country followed her lead when she stopped wearing a bustle on her skirts. Oh, the rebelliousness of youth! Who was she?

(a) Mary Arthur McElroy

(b) Frances Folsom Cleveland

(c) Helen Herron Taft

(d) Hilary Houston Bachelder

A N S W E R

The answer is **(b)**: Grover Cleveland's child bride is also the only First Lady to serve two nonconsecutive terms—with or without a bustle.

41 Which notable First Lady graduated with a degree in geology from Stanford University, spoke five languages, including Chinese, and worked with her husband to translate a book on mining from Latin called *De Re Metallica*, originally published in 1556?

(a) Jacqueline Bouvier Kennedy

(b) Sarah Childress Polk

(c) Lou Henry Hoover

(d) Eleanor Roosevelt

ANSWER

(c). Lou Henry Hoover was the First Lady of formidable talents.

42 Just after her husband took office, Jacqueline Kennedy began a campaign of her own: a historic restoration of the White House, to make it a showcase of American history and art. The Kennedy restoration was an enormous success, even more remarkable because no public funds were used. She accomplished it with private donations, gifts of art, and profits from a White House guidebook. Her work led to a special award for Mrs. Kennedy, who was the only First Lady to receive it. During which awards ceremony was she honored?

(a) Pulitzer prizes

(b) Academy awards

(c) Emmy awards

(d) U.N. Medal of Honor ceremony

ANSWER

The answer is **(c)**: Jacqueline Kennedy was given a Special Trustees award during the Emmy ceremonies for hosting a televised tour of the White House in 1962.

We've had some great orators in the Oval Office, so we're calling the next set of questions The Wit and Wisdom. We'll provide the bon mot; you tell us who said it.

43 "I am a great lover of humor, however little I have of it." Which optimistic, lighthearted leader was speaking?

(a) Calvin Coolidge

(b) Chester A. Arthur

(c) William Howard Taft

(d) Rutherford B. Hayes

43

ANSWER

(c). Taft.

44 And who said: "I may be the president of the United States, but my private life is my own damned business"?

(a) Bill Clinton

(b) Richard Nixon

(c) Ronald Reagan

(d) Chester A. Arthur

A N S W E R

(d). The more things change, the more they stay the same. Although a case could be made for any of the above, "Elegant" Chester A. Arthur is the one credited with this particular bon mot.

45 What about this one: "When the president does it, it means that it is not illegal"? Let's go with the same choices, shall we?

(a) Bill Clinton

(b) Richard Nixon

(c) Ronald Reagan

(d) Chester A. Arthur

ANSWER

The answer is **(b)**. This time it was Tricky Dick who uttered the above words.

46 Which U.S. president reportedly said: "I know what I am fit for. I can command a body of men in a rough way, but I am not fit to be president"?

(a) Andrew Jackson

(b) William Henry Harrison

(c) Theodore Roosevelt

(d) Dwight D. Eisenhower

46

ANSWER

(a). Andrew Jackson, the seventh president of the United States and a hero of the War of 1812, came up with that one.

47 Upon receiving an honorary degree from Yale, which president said: "Now ... I have the best of both worlds, a Harvard education and a Yale degree"?

(a) John Adams

(b) John Quincy Adams

(c) Franklin Roosevelt

(d) John F. Kennedy

A N S W E R

This quote is attributed to **(d)** John F. Kennedy, the last president to graduate from Harvard University.

Let's take trip to Mount Rushmore, the set of largest presidential portraits in the world. it took fourteen years to complete; about six and a half years of actual work and the rest of the time spent looking for funding and waiting for the weather to break. The answers to the next five questions are to be found in the faces of the four men on the mountain.

 48 Who was the only president to receive a patent for an invention?

(a) Washington

(b) Jefferson

(c) Roosevelt

(d) Lincoln

48

(d). Abraham Lincoln was the first and only U.S. president to obtain a patent, which he received in 1849. He invented a device to help large boats pass through shallow waters.

49 Which president appointed the greatest number of Supreme Court Justices?

(a) Washington

(b) Jefferson

(c) Roosevelt

(d) Lincoln

A N S W E R

The answer is **(a)** George Washington. You see, you had to start somewhere, and he appointed eleven Justices to the Supreme Court.

50 Okay, this has nothing to do with Mount Rushmore, but while we're on the topic: Which man was the only one to actually be appointed as a Justice to the Supreme Court?

(a) Rutherford B. Hayes

(b) Chester A. Arthur

(c) William Howard Taft

(d) Warren G. Harding

50

ANSWER

(c). Harding appointed Taft the Chief Justice of the United States. Taft, in fact, swore in two presidents himself: Calvin Coolidge and Herbert Hoover were both sworn in by the former president.

51 Back to the mountain: This man was one of only two men who served the United States as secretary of state, vice president, and president. Who was he?

(a) Washington

(b) Jefferson

(c) Roosevelt

(d) Lincoln

A N S W E R

The answer is **(b)** Thomas Jefferson. The other guy who did all that was Martin Van Buren.

Most presidents are human. And because they're human, they can fall victim to the same temptations as the rest of us. Here is our salute to scandals at the White House.

52 Okay, before we get into the sex, lies, and audiotape of presidential scandals, let's begin with a warmup question. You probably know that two U.S. presidents have been impeached—but how many presidents were actually arrested while in office?

(a) 0

(b) 1

(c) 2

(d) 4

A N S W E R

The answer is **(c)**. Two presidents have been arrested while in office, and both incidents involved horses in Washington, D.C. Before your imaginations run away with you, here's the story: Franklin Pierce was busted after running down an old woman with his horse, but the case was later dropped. And Ulysses S. Grant was at the reins when he was arrested for speeding in his horse and buggy.

53 Twenty years before Watergate, vice-presidential candidate Richard Nixon faced a nearly career-ending scandal. Accused of misusing monies from a secret fund, Nixon was about to be dropped by his running mate, Dwight Eisenhower. But he survived by giving an extraordinary address on TV and radio that has become known as the "Checkers speech." Your question: What was Nixon referring to when he spoke of Checkers?

(a) His pet dog

(b) Dirty political games

(c) His version of the "domino theory"

(d) The game he enjoyed playing with his family

ANSWER

The answer is **(a)**. Checkers was the name of the family dog. In his emotional speech, Nixon denied misusing funds but admitted accepting a dog as a gift to his children. "Regardless of what they say," stated Nixon firmly, "we're gonna keep it." His speech won over the public and convinced Eisenhower to keep him on the ticket. Lucky for Nixon, Checkers turned down the vice presidency.

54 From Iran-contragate to Zippergate, and every disgrace in between, one name represents the mother of all presidential scandals: Watergate. We know what happened and how it all ended, but the question is this: Which group planned the break-in at the Democratic headquarters in the Watergate hotel complex?

(a) CREEP
(Committee to Re-Elect the President)

(b) DORK
(Defenders of the Republican King)

(c) CRUD
(Covert Republicans Undermining Democrats)

(d) DARN
(Dedicated Army of Republican Nationalists)

ANSWER

The answer is **(a)** the Committee to Re-Elect the President, which was known by the all-too-fitting acronym CREEP. G. Gordon Liddy and E. Howard Hunt were members, as was former attorney general John Mitchell. All of them served time in prison for their crimes.

55 Ronald Reagan earned the nickname "the Teflon president" because none of the controversies or problems that erupted during his administration ever seemed to stick to him. During the Iran-contra affair, the problems all fell upon one man—the only man to have stood trial for his role in the arms scandal. His name?

(a) Oliver North

(b) Robert McFarlane

(c) William Buckley

(d) John Tower

ANSWER

(a). Oliver North was the only man to stand trial for his role in the Iran-contra affair.

56 As incendiary in its time as the Iran-contra affair was in the late 1980s, the Teapot Dome scandal rocked the nation when it came to the public's attention in 1923. What exactly was the Teapot Dome scandal all about?

(a) The selling of military secrets to the Germans

(b) The steel strike of 1919

(c) Federal oil reserves in Wyoming and California

(d) The illegal taxing of tea by the House of Representatives

56

ANSWER

(c). The Teapot Dome scandal was one of many scandals to plague Warren G. Harding's presidency. Teapot Dome, Wyoming, was one of two federal oil reserves that interior secretary Albert Fall leased to private drilling companies in exchange for kickbacks. After the scandal was uncovered, Fall became the first cabinet officer in American history to go to jail.

57 Bill Clinton has the unfortunate distinction of being one of two presidents who were impeached by the House of Representatives—and it will be a long while before we all forget why. But perhaps it won't be too long at all: Do you recall why Andrew Johnson was impeached?

(a) Failing to account for the $7 million used to purchase Alaska

(b) For being in violation of the Tenure of Office Act by removing the secretary of war from office

(c) For conspiring with Secretary of State William Seward to undermine Congress's opposition to the Fourteenth Amendment

(d) For overstepping the boundaries of the judicial branch by granting full pardon to Jefferson Davis

(b). Although there were a number of charges brought against Johnson during the impeachment, the majority of them focused on his violating the Tenure of Office Act.

58 President Clinton's escapade with Monica Lewinsky actually wasn't the first sex scandal to rock the White House. In fact, one of our founding fathers found himself embroiled in a sex scandal early on in our nation's history: He was accused of fathering an illegitimate child with one of his slaves, a woman by the name of Sally Hemings. Which president was this?

(a) Abraham Lincoln

(b) Thomas Jefferson

(c) John Adams

(d) George Washington

58

ANSWER

(b). During his presidency, a rumor developed that Thomas Jefferson had fathered several illegitimate children with Sally Hemings, one of his slaves. Although this claim has been hotly debated, two independent tests in the late 1990s indicate that Jefferson was almost certainly the father of Eston Hemings, one of Sally's sons.

When Teddy Roosevelt took office, his five youngest children literally turned the White House into Animal House. Their menagerie included a bear, a badger, raccoons, cats, rats, dogs, snakes, guinea pigs, and a calico pony named Algonquin. Let's recover from the presidential scandals with a few heartwarming questions about presidential pets.

59 In the midst of the Revolutionary War, a lost dog strayed into General Washington's army camp. The American soldiers soon discovered that the dog belonged to their sworn enemy, British general Sir William Howe—Howe's name was engraved right on the dog's collar. The question is: What did George Washington do with the dog?

(a) Exchanged him for POWs

(b) Returned him under a flag of truce

(c) Executed him by firing squad

(d) Held him ransom for military intelligence

59

The answer is **(b)**: The dog was returned under a flag of truce. Washington himself owned many dogs for foxhunting, and he surely sympathized with General Howe's loss. With the dog safely returned, Washington and his troops could get back to the job of trying to kill the dog's owner and his men.

60 In an incredibly strange and tragic coincidence, one presidential pet was actually murdered just a short while after his master was assassinated. Who were the president and the pet?

(a) Abraham Lincoln and his dog Fido

(b) James Garfield and his cat Whiskers

(c) William McKinley and his dog Trooper

(d) John F. Kennedy and his dog Clipper

ANSWER

The answer is **(a)** Abraham Lincoln and his dog Fido. Within a year after Lincoln's assassination, his beloved Fido was killed by an angry drunk after the dog had put his dirty paws on him.

61 Believe it or not, at the height of the Cold War, an American and a Russian got together and conceived babies in the White House. The American was none other than the president's dog Charlie. He sired puppies born to Pushinka, a Russian dog given to the president's daughter by the premier of the Soviet Union. Your question: Name the U.S. president and Soviet premier who brought about this historic mating.

(a) Eisenhower and Khrushchev

(b) Kennedy and Khrushchev

(c) Nixon and Brezhnev

(d) Carter and Brezhnev

61

ANSWER

The answer is **(b)**. To ease tensions after the Cuban Missile Crisis, Nikita Khrushchev gave Pushinka to John F. Kennedy's daughter, Caroline. Pushinka and Charlie had four puppies together, which President Kennedy called "pupniks."

62 Which president gave his grand-children a goat by the name of His Whiskers?

(a) Benjamin Harrison

(b) Zachary Taylor

(c) James Buchanan

(d) Ulysses S. Grant

ANSWER

(a). His Whiskers was the name of the goat Benjamin Harrison gave to his grandchildren. In a famous story, now part of White House lore, President Harrison once had to chase His Whiskers down Pennsylvania Avenue when the goat broke free of the White House gates!

63 And which president's favorite pet was a racoon named Rebecca?

(a) Dwight D. Eisenhower

(b) Harry Truman

(c) Franklin Roosevelt

(d) Calvin Coolidge

63

ANSWER

Rebecca was the beloved pet of **(d)** Calvin Coolidge and his wife, Grace. President Coolidge could often be seen walking his precious pet around the White House on a leash. In fact, the Coolidges were so well known for their love of animals that they received animals from all over the world as gifts: cats, dogs, birds, a baby bear, antelopes, a pygmy hippo, and a bobcat were just some of the animals sent to the White House during the Coolidge administration.

64 One of the most famous presidential pooches was FDR's faithful Scottish terrier, who was present when FDR and Winston Churchill signed the Atlantic Charter in 1941. At the Franklin Delano Roosevelt memorial in Washington, D.C., a statue of this dog was erected right next to his beloved master. A biography of this famous dog was written by Margaret Suckley, FDR's cousin. The question: What was the name of this powerful pup?

(a) Macaroni

(b) Dee-Dee

(c) Lincoln

(d) Fala

64

ANSWER

(d). Fala was the name of FDR's constant canine companion.

65 But Fala wasn't the only dog to take pen to paw and write a book. Which First Lady helped her springer spaniel Millie write a best-selling book?

(a) Lady Bird Johnson

(b) Barbara Bush

(c) Nancy Reagan

(d) Hillary Clinton

65

The answer is **(b)**. "Dictated" to Barbara Bush, *Millie's Book* was a #1 *New York Times* best-seller when it was published in 1990.

Some presidential scandals are serious and far reaching. Others are inconsequential and embarrassing but get lots of attention anyway. This category is about the latter, and we call it Oaf of Office.

66 This president had a pretty dignified image until he fell out of his chair and threw up at a Japanese state dinner. Who was it?

(a) Ronald Reagan

(b) George Bush

(c) Jimmy Carter

(d) Gerald Ford

A N S W E R

The answer is **(b)** George Bush. I guess he had too much sukiyaki that night.

67 Only a Democrat would lower himself to this next exhibition of presidential bad taste. You see, this chief executive showed his gallbladder scar to TV reporters and photographers. Who was it?

(a) Lyndon B. Johnson

(b) John F. Kennedy

(c) Harry Truman

(d) Franklin Roosevelt

A N S W E R

The answer is **(a)** Lyndon Baines Johnson.

68 Now, golfing is serious business, so when squirrels showed up on the White House putting green of this president, he ordered a sergeant to shoot the cute little buggers. Who gave that order?

(a) Dwight D. Eisenhower

(b) Harry Truman

(c) Calvin Coolidge

(d) Warren G. Harding

A N S W E R

The animal lover was **(a)** Dwight D. Eisenhower.

Here are a few questions that separate some presidents from the rest of the pack. We'll call this next section of questions You're My One and Only.

 69 Who was the only president to have two vice presidents die in office?

(a) James Monroe

(b) James Madison

(c) Andrew Jackson

(d) John Tyler

69

ANSWER

The unlucky president was **(b)** James Madison. George Clinton and Elbridge Gerry both died in office. Good help can be hard to find.

70 Who was the only president not to have a vice president?

(a) George Washington

(b) Thomas Jefferson

(c) John Tyler

(d) Calvin Coolidge

70

(c). When John Tyler took over the presidency after the death of William Henry Harrison, he kept Harrison's cabinet but never got around to naming a new vice president. The constitutional provision for replacing a vice president did not come into effect until the ratification of the Twenty-fifth Amendment in 1967.

71 Who was the only president to be president for a day?

(a) Thomas E. Dewey

(b) Henry A. Wallace

(c) Wendell Wilkie

(d) David Rice Atchison

A N S W E R

America's twelfth president was actually a man named **(d)** David Rice Atchison. James K. Polk's administration officially ended on March 3, 1849. But since Zachary Taylor was such a devout Episcopalian he refused to be sworn in on a Sunday, David Rice Atchison, president pro tempore of the Senate, was officially the president of the United States on March 4, 1849.

72 Who was the only president who never married?

(a) John Tyler

(b) James Buchanan

(c) Grover Cleveland

(d) Benjamin Harrison

72

ANSWER

(b). James Buchanan was our only bachelor president. Though Grover Cleveland was a bachelor when he was elected to the White House, he became the first elected president to marry in the White House when he wed Frances Folsom on June 2, 1886. John Tyler has the distinction of being the first president to both lose his wife and then get married again while in office.

73 Fifteen presidents have thrown out the first ball on Opening Day of major-league baseball seasons on fifty-five occasions. Since William H. Taft began this tradition in 1910, only one president has never thrown out the first ball. Who was this poor sport?

(a) Bill Clinton

(b) George Bush

(c) Ronald Reagan

(d) Jimmy Carter

73

ANSWER

(d). Although he threw out a few first balls for the Atlanta Braves while he was governor of Georgia, Jimmy Carter never threw out the first ball of the season as president.

This next set of questions is a kind of grab bag of some presidential questions we thought you'd find interesting . . .

74 With pensions and money from speeches and books, U.S. presidents now enjoy a secure retirement—but this wasn't always the case. Thomas Jefferson, for example, enjoyed living large, and was already in debt when he left the presidency. His free-spending ways continued, however, and at the age of eighty-three, Jefferson wrote that he didn't even have the cash to buy groceries. What scheme did Jefferson then devise to raise money?

(a) Sell duplicates of the Declaration of Independence

(b) Offer his beloved Monticello as the grand prize in a lottery

(c) Begin bottling TJ—his own brand of fine wine

(d) Charge for lectures and appearances

ANSWER

The answer is **(b)**. But poor ticket sales made his lottery scheme a bust, so friends sought donations to get him out of debt. Sadly, this effort failed too, and Jefferson died soon afterward. Monticello was then auctioned to help pay his creditors.

75 The headline that incorrectly proclaimed "Dewey Defeats Truman!" is perhaps one of the most famous journalistic gaffes of the twentieth century. The question is: What paper printed this egregious headline?

(a) *Dallas Morning News*

(b) *New York Times*

(c) *Chicago Tribune*

(d) *San Francisco Chronicle*

A N S W E R

(c). The *Chicago Tribune* printed the now famous headline.

76 Right may make might, but lefties have had their share of power too. Which of the following presidents were not left-handed?

(a) George Bush

(b) Bill Clinton

(c) Ronald Reagan

(d) Gerald Ford

A N S W E R

(c). There have been five left-handed presidents in our nation's history, but President Ronald Reagan was not one of them. The other southpaws were James Garfield and Harry Truman.

77 Who was in office when Colorado became a state, Alexander Graham Bell made the first phone call, and Mrs. O'Leary's cow supposedly lit Chicago afire?

(a) Ulysses S. Grant (1869–1877)

(b) Benjamin Harrison (1889–1893)

(c) William McKinley (1897–1901)

(d) James A. Garfield (1880)

ANSWER

The answer is **(a)**. Although the story of Mrs. O'Leary's cow is a legend, there's no doubt that Ulysses S. Grant was president at the time of the Chicago fire in 1871.

78 In dire circumstances, retired presidents are sometimes called upon to use their influence and diplomatic skills to resolve conflicts. Such was the case in 1985, when the tensions between two warring factions threatened to boil over and consume our nation. On one side of the battle was major-league baseball; on the other side was the MLB Umpire Association. Name the former U.S. president who mediated a peaceful contract settlement between the two groups.

(a) Richard Nixon

(b) Gerald Ford

(c) Jimmy Carter

(d) Dwight D. Eisenhower

78

ANSWER

The answer is **(a)**. Richard Nixon was a big baseball fan, and he was asked to arbitrate the dispute by a friend, who was head of the Umpire Association. Both sides then agreed to his appointment. There is NO truth to the rumor that a botched break-in at the head-quarters of major-league baseball forced Nixon to resign this position.

We're on the home stretch here, time to score those all-important final points. This next group of questions features some spicy presidential quotations. We'll read the quote; you decide who said it.

79 "I've just read your lousy review of Margaret's concert. I've come to the conclusion you are an eight ulcer man on four ulcer pay. . . . Some day, I hope to meet you. When that happens, you'll need a new nose, a lot of beefsteak for black eyes, and perhaps a supporter below!" Which president is quoted?

(a) Harry Truman

(b) Lyndon B. Johnson

(c) Gerald Ford

(d) Rutherford B. Hayes

79

ANSWER

The answer is **(a)** Harry Truman. Margaret was his daughter, an aspiring opera singer. And Harry obviously didn't mince words with the guy who reviewed Margaret's concert.

80 Here's the next quote: "Richard Nixon is a no-good lying bastard. He can lie out of both sides of his mouth at the same time, and if he ever caught himself telling the truth, he'd lie just to keep his hand in." Which president said it?

(a) John F. Kennedy

(b) Jimmy Carter

(c) Harry Truman

(d) Lyndon B. Johnson

ANSWER

(c). Once again, the answer is Harry Truman. Gotta love Harry Truman: He didn't hold back; he spoke his mind.

81 Which president said: "Ike didn't know anything, and all the time he was in office he didn't learn a thing"?

(a) John F. Kennedy

(b) Harry Truman

(c) Richard Nixon

(d) Lyndon B. Johnson

81

A N S W E R

Yup, the answer to this question is **(b)**.
Harry Truman strikes again.

Like most American citizens, presidents occasionally consume food. Here are some questions about the first appetite.

82 President Franklin Roosevelt ruffled some feathers in the international press corps when he served the king and queen of England a simple, all-American meal. What controversial cuisine did Roosevelt deem fit for a king?

(a) Hot dogs

(b) Cheeseburgers

(c) Sloppy Joes

(d) Hamburgers and French fries

82

A N S W E R

The answer is **(a)**. Roosevelt served hot dogs on buns to King George VI and Queen Elizabeth. Apparently, the royals and the wieners got along just fine, though the queen was a bit perplexed about how to eat them: She used a knife and fork instead of her hands.

83 You might call the president the Big Cheese of American government. But there have literally been some mighty big cheeses in the White House over the years. A dairy farmer once sent Andrew Jackson a 1,400-pound cheddar cheese as a gift. It traveled from New York to Washington on a flag-draped wagon pulled by twenty-four horses! Jackson let the cheese age, then made a plan to share his fabulous fromage. What did Jackson do?

(a) Served the cheese at a joint session of Congress

(b) Shipped a piece of cheese to every nation on earth

(c) Make a mold from the cheese and erected a statue on the White House lawn

(d) Publicly invited everyone to eat cheese at the White House

83

A N S W E R

The answer is **(d)**. Jackson actually published an open invitation and—not surprisingly—a huge mob showed up at the White House. Chaos erupted and cheese was scattered all over the White House floor and furniture, as the party spilled outside. So, thanks to a bunch of rowdy cheeseheads, you probably won't be getting invited back to the White House any time soon.

84 George Bush was also famous for his eating habits. So much so that he once made a speech and officially declared: "I am the president of the United States. And I am not going to eat any more _____."

(a) Jellybeans

(b) Cauliflower

(c) Broccoli

(d) Potatoes

84

ANSWER

(c). Bush had a noted dislike for broccoli and wasn't ashamed to admit it. His veep, J. Danforth Quayle, also had a well-publicized dislike for the spelling of the word *potato*, but that's another question.

The next three questions feature three zippy little programs devised by U.S. presidents. We'll name the program, you figure out who instituted it. Which president was responsible for:

85 The New Deal?

(a) Franklin Roosevelt

(b) John F. Kennedy

(c) Dwight D. Eisenhower

(d) Harry Truman

A N S W E R

The New Deal was the brainchild of **(a)** Franklin Roosevelt.

86 The Great Society?

(a) John F. Kennedy

(b) Lyndon B. Johnson

(c) Richard Nixon

(d) Dwight D. Eisenhower

86

(b). The Great Society is the name given to the domestic program of U.S. president Lyndon B. Johnson. The Great Society was defined in Johnson's 1965 State of the Union speech as one in which federally sponsored programs would improve the quality of life for all Americans.

87 A Thousand Points of Light?

(a) Jimmy Carter

(b) Ronald Reagan

(c) George Bush

(d) Bill Clinton

A N S W E R

(c). When George Bush accepted his party's nomination for the presidency in 1988, he described America as "a brilliant diversity spread like stars, like a thousand points of light in a broad and peaceful sky." Later, in his inauguration speech, he further defined "the thousand points of light" as individual people who give of themselves to make America a better place to live.

Sometimes American history can get kind of confusing. As if it isn't difficult enough to figure out how the Electoral College works, we wind up with not one but two presidents named Roosevelt. Just to straighten things out, your job is to figure out if the following statements apply to Theodore Roosevelt, Franklin Delano Roosevelt, or both.

 His wife and his mother died on the same day.

ANSWER

Theodore Roosevelt. His first wife, Alice Lee Roosevelt, died on the same day as his mother in 1884.

89 He proclaimed that "The only thing we have to fear is fear itself."

ANSWER

Franklin Delano Roosevelt came up with this oft-quoted proverb in his 1933 inaugural address.

90 He implemented Social Security.

90

ANSWER

Social Security was the brainchild of **Franklin D. Roosevelt.**

91
He graduated from Harvard University.

A N S W E R

Both Roosevelts graduated from Harvard. Theodore graduated magna cum laude from Harvard in 1880; Franklin graduated in 1903.

92 He was a Republican.

ANSWER

Teddy was the Republican of the Roosevelt family.

93 He was once the governor of New York.

ANSWER

Both Roosevelts served terms as governor of New York: Theodore Roosevelt was elected governor in 1898; Franklin followed suit in 1928.

When it comes to presidential politics, money talks. Here's proof:

 94 The question is: What bill carries President Grant's furry face?

(a) $50

(b) $100

(c) $500

(d) $10,000

ANSWER

The answer is **(a)**. President Grant's face graces the $50 bill.

95 The very first secretary of the U.S. Treasury is also pictured on a bill. Who is it, and what bill is he featured on?

(a) Alexander Hamilton ($10)

(b) James Madison ($1,000)

(c) John Kennedy ($5,000)

(d) Salmon P. Chase ($10,000)

95

ANSWER

If you chose **(a)** Hamilton and the $10 bill, you're right on the money.

The Secret Service is envied as the group that gets to come up with cool code names for the president. Here are a few questions about the real goings-on inside this most elite of the government's agencies:

 96 What was the original function of the Secret Service?

(a) To suppress counterfeit currency

(b) To prevent illegal immigration

(c) To prevent illegal importation of farm goods from other countries

(d) To monitor the building of the Transcontinental Railroad

96

(a). The Secret Service Division began on July 5, 1865, in Washington, D.C., to suppress counterfeit currency. Two years later, the job was expanded to include "detecting persons perpetuating frauds against the government."

97 In what year did the Secret Service formally assume full-time responsibility for the president's safety and well-being?

(a) 1902

(b) 1914

(c) 1917

(d) 1976

97

(a). Although they had informally protected President Cleveland and President Roosevelt after McKinley's assassination, the Secret Service did not officially begin protecting the president until 1902, when two operatives were assigned to the White House to protect Teddy Roosevelt.

98 Which of the following people do not receive Secret Service protection under the current law?

(a) The president's daughter

(b) The vice presidential candidate from a major party

(c) The visiting head of a foreign state

(d) The vice president's spouse

98

(d). The vice president's wife isn't eligible for Secret Service protection. As the law stands now, the Secret Service protects the president, the First Family, the president-elect, the vice president, the vice president-elect, all visiting heads of state and their spouses, and the major presidential and vice presidential candidates and nominees.

99 How long does a former president receive the protection of the Secret Service?

(a) Six months

(b) One year

(c) Ten years

(d) Lifetime

99

ANSWER

Actually, this was a trick question. The answer is: It depends. All presidents elected to office after January 1, 1997, will receive Secret Service protection for ten years after leaving office. Individuals elected to office before that date receive lifetime protection.

100 And here's a question about our forty-third president, George W. Bush: He's obviously related to his presidential father. But to which other president is George W. Bush related?

(a) William Howard Taft

(b) Franklin Pierce

(c) Grover Cleveland

(d) Warren G. Harding

100

A N S W E R

(b). Barbara Pierce Bush is (follow us closely now) a fourth cousin four times removed of President Franklin Pierce. That makes George W. Bush and Franklin Pierce . . . well . . . distantly related.

101 The good news: You've just completed almost every question in this edition of *The Great American History Quiz.* The bad news: We left out one president—one leader of our nation who never made it into a question or an answer. It's up to you to identify this hero of Buffalo, New York, whose number on the list of presidents is unlucky 13. Who did we leave out?

(a) Franklin Pierce

(b) Chester A. Arthur

(c) Millard Fillmore

(d) Rutherford B. Hayes

101

The answer is **(c)** Millard Fillmore. Sorry, Millie.